Anthem How To Do
11+ and 12+ Verbal Reasoning

ANTHEM LEARNING VERBAL REASONING

A comprehensive and practical guide to verbal reasoning, this series is an indispensable tool for pupils looking to clear their 11+ and 12+ verbal reasoning exams. Written by experienced tutors, the **Anthem Learning Verbal Reasoning** series offers extensive coverage of the types of problems featured in examinations, including clear, step-by-step instructions on how to solve them. With its useful tips on how to prepare for tests, as well as its wide range of practice materials, the **Anthem Learning Verbal Reasoning** series is a vital resource both for beginners and experienced students.

The series includes a **How To Do** guide on technique and questions likely to be asked, as well as an array of practice and test papers. The **Test Papers** in multiple-choice format can be used to emulate exam conditions, and offer a wide variety of increasingly difficult problems that will challenge pupils of all abilities. Meanwhile, the **Short Revision Papers** in multiple-choice format can be used to pinpoint weak spots and areas for further work, and are perfect for students looking to top up their skills – and for those with busy schedules.

Designed to instil confidence, the **Anthem Learning Verbal Reasoning** series is ideal for those sitting verbal reasoning exams or looking to hone their communication skills, and will be an invaluable resource for students and parents alike.

PUBLISHED BY ANTHEM PRESS

75–76 Blackfriars Road, London SE1 8HA, UK
or PO Box 9779, London SW19 7ZG, UK

ISBN-13: 978 0 85728 382 5 (Pbk)
ISBN-10: 0 85728 382 0 (Pbk)

This title is also available as an eBook.

Anthem How To Do 11+ and 12+ Verbal Reasoning

Technique and Practice

John Connor and Pat Soper

ANTHEM PRESS
LONDON · NEW YORK · DELHI

Table of Contents

Introduction

Verbal reasoning tests are increasingly used as a tool for assessing a child's educational potential. Indeed, the majority of schools include verbal reasoning papers as part, in some instances wholly, of their assessment procedures. Analysis of such papers demonstrates the validity of such an approach. Papers test a whole range of competences including ability to solve problems, process information, think logically and to follow and determine patterns and rules.

An important feature of verbal reasoning tests is a pupil's ability to work systematically against the clock. It is important to realise from the outset that the crucial determinant in gaining success is the number of questions answered correctly. That is, in a paper comprising 100 questions, a score of 79 correctly answered questions out of 80 completed is a less good result than a score of 80 correctly answered out of 100 completed questions – although the former score is a higher percentage of correct answers. Since time is therefore critical, a candidate must be familiar with the most common questions and must possess a strategy on how best to approach each type.

A range of verbal reasoning papers has been analysed and the contents have been broken down into major types. In this book, each type has been allocated a separate chapter. Each chapter follows the same pattern and comprises:

1. The type of question is described, including an example. This is important since it is essential to have a clear idea of what is required.

2. A suggested strategy is given. In many cases, of course, there are different approaches to answering the questions, but the approaches given in the book have been well tried and successfully applied over many years.

3. A number of worked examples are included allowing the candidate to be totally familiar with the suggested strategy.

4. Each chapter concludes with a number of questions on the type. All the questions have been pre-tested to ensure a high degree of validity.

To maximize the value of the programme the following stages might be followed:

i. Ensure that you have a clear understanding of each type of question.

ii. Study the hints that are suggested in each chapter, acquiring a strategy that best suits your needs.

iii. Follow the hints given in the worked examples, making sure that you have a clear idea as to how the correct answer has been achieved.

iv. Tackle the questions on each type. Check your own answer and work from the answer provided at the back of the book to appreciate where you may have gone wrong.

When each type has been studied then full verbal reasoning papers can be attempted. Candidates will be able to approach papers with a high degree of confidence. Naturally, the more papers completed by the student will result in greater confidence and, equally importantly, speed will be increased.

It is important to appreciate that very few candidates achieve 100% success, and that certain types of questions might be found to be more difficult than others.

Unit 1. Transferring Letters

In this type of question, you are given two words. You are required to move one letter from the word on the left, leaving a new word. Then insert the letter removed into the word on the right, again creating a new word. When inserting this letter, it can be placed anywhere in the word on the right.

For example: COULD   BOND

      By removing U from COULD a new word is formed: COLD.

      By inserting U into BOND a new word is formed: BOUND.

Hints

i.   The letter must be removed from the word on the left.

ii.   Remember the letters cannot be rearranged.

iii.   Ensure the words created are sensible. (A good guide is to ask yourself if you have written the word previously or have come across it in your reading.)

iv.   Proper nouns are not to be given as answers – for example, names of people, cities and so on.

Worked Examples

1.   FEAR   SPED

By removing the letter E from FEAR, we make FAR and by inserting the E after the P we make SPEED.

Answer: FAR   SPEED

2.   PART   DUG

By removing the letter R from PART, we make PAT and by inserting the R after the D we make DRUG.

Answer: PAT   DRUG

3.   FLOOD   PET

By removing the letter L from FLOOD, we make FOOD and by inserting the L after the E we make PELT.

Answer: FOOD   PELT

Practice Questions

In the following questions, move one letter from the left hand word and put the letter into the right hand word to make two new words.

1. DROOP   MAN   _____   _____

2. HOARSE   VENUE   _____   _____

3. PAINT   EAR   _____   _____

4. NONE   EITHER   _____   _____

5. FLAME   SIGHT   _____   _____

6. CLIMB   SENT   _____   _____

7. CLAP   SIP   _____   _____

8. TRIP   BID   _____   _____

9. COAT   BAT   _____   _____

10. SCENT   ARE   _____   _____

11. PLANT   CAME   _____   _____

12. BLACK   BET   _____   _____

13. CARD   SHE   _____   _____

14. CEASE   POT   _____   _____

15. WRING   GASP   _____   _____

16. PAID   PAL   _____   _____

17. MANY   SAD   _____   _____

18 THANK SORE _____ _____

19 FLOG FEW _____ _____

20 RING TOW _____ _____

Unit 2. Missing Letters

In this type of question, you are required to find a letter which completes one word and begins another. You are given two pairs of incomplete words and are required to choose a letter that fits both pairs.

These questions can be set out in different ways.

For example: PIL ( ) AST   :   RIC ( ) AR   or   PIL ? AST
RIC ? AR

The answer is E to make PILE EAST   :   RICE EAR

In many instances the missing letter is obvious. If this is not the case, the following hints may help.

Hints

i.   In the absence of an alphabet, write one on the paper.

ii.   Select the first incomplete word and, by logically going through the alphabet, find a letter which, when added, makes a sensible word.

iii.   Determine whether that letter, when put in front of the second group of letters, again makes a sensible word.

iv.   Then determine whether the same letter both ends and starts the second pair.

v.   If it is found that the selected letter does not achieve this, go back to the first incomplete word and choose another letter.

Worked Example

RIC ( ) ATS   :   SUC ( ) ARE

1.   By looking at RIC and going through the alphabet, the first letter to make a sensible word is E, to make RICE. This letter also begins the word EATS.

2.   When coming to the second pair, the letter E added to SUC does not form a correct word.

3. Referring back to the first word, the next letter making a sensible word is H – RICH and HATS.

4. When applied to SUC this now makes SUCH and HARE.

Answer: H

Practice Questions

In each of the questions below, find <u>one</u> letter that will complete the word in front of the brackets and begin the word after the brackets.

The <u>same</u> letter must complete both sets of words.

A B C D E F G H I J K L M N O P Q R S T U V W X Y Z

1. KIN ( ) ARK : TREN ( ) ANCE

2. SIG ( ) OTE : PLA ( ) ATION

3. FLE ( ) AR : THA ( ) ITCH

4. SOL ( ) RANGE : PIAN ( ) RBIT

5. STA ( ) OKE : ST ( ) AWN

6. PLU ( ) AME : BAN ( ) RIEF

7. SOR ( ) EMPLE : SAL ( ) ASTE

8. RAC ( ) EY : FOR ( ) ICK

9. DEA ( ) OCK : STEE ( ) IMP

10. DEE ( ) ARK : MIN ( ) OSE

11. SCAR ( ) ALSE : FLUF ( ) ADE

12. IDEA ( ) OFT : REE ( ) UNG

13. REA ( ) EEK : PLU ( ) ARK

14. HI ( ) OUR : SNA ( ) URE

15. SLO ( ) OMB : CAR ( ) ILE

16 MAI ( ) AWN : BLEN ( ) EAD

17 HEA ( ) HATCH : THREA ( ) HEN

18 RAI ( ) UMP : BEL ( ) ORD

19 SKI ( ) ONE : STU ( ) OVEL

20 PLU ( ) ANGER : STE ( ) AIN

Unit 3. Letter Series

In this type of question, you are given a series of letters and are required to find the next letter or letters in the series. (You are normally given the alphabet but, if not, it is a good idea to write it out.)

A B C D E F G H I J K L M N O P Q R S T U V W X Y Z

For example: A C E G __

Hints

i.   Look to see if the letters are ascending or descending in reasonably small intervals. Write in the number of moves from one letter to the next in the series and you will usually find a pattern. For example: going from A to D is three moves.

A B C D
3

Simply continue the pattern. Use '+' for going forward and '-' for going back. So –

A $^{+2}$ C $^{+2}$ E $^{+2}$ G $^{+2}$ I
  ^   ^   ^   ^

Look to see if the letters are ascending or descending at larger intervals.
In this case, the moves between the letters are increasing.

A $^{+2}$ C $^{+3}$ F $^{+4}$ J $^{+5}$ O
  ^   ^   ^   ^

ii.   If the letters are going up and down alternately, then the series is probably what might be called a 'jumper'.

B   Z   D   X   F   V   H __ __

Once you realise it's a jumper then start at the first letter and jump to the third, the fifth and so on following the method above. Then return to the second letter and jump to the fourth and so on.

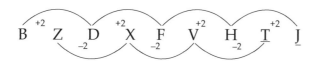

B $^{+2}$ Z D $^{+2}$ X F $^{+2}$ V H $^{+2}$ T J
      -2   -2   -2

iii. It is important in a jumper that the letter you give as the answer is from the correct series.

iv. Occasionally there are two (or more) letters together.

> BS   DQ   FO   HM   ___

Treat each letter as a separate series in the following manner:

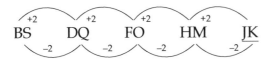

v. Imagine the alphabet forms a circle. The letter A comes after Z. Therefore, Z plus 2 moves is B and, similarly, C minus 4 moves is Y.

Worked Examples

1.   A   D   G   J   M   ___

   A⁺³   D⁺³   G⁺³   J⁺³   M⁺³   P
   ^   ^   ^   ^   ^

2.   Z   X   U   Q   ___

   Z⁻²   X⁻³   U⁻⁴   Q⁻⁵   L
        ^   ^   ^   ^

3.   A   Z   C   X   E   V   ___   ___

   A   Z   C   X   E   V   G   T

   Note: The answer is G T, not T G.

4.   FJ   GH   IF   LD   ___

   FJ   GH   IF   LD   PB

Practice Questions

In the following questions, you need to find the letter or letters that will continue the series.

A B C D E F G H I J K L M N O P Q R S T U V W X Y Z

1 B D F H J ___

2 R P N L J ___

3 A B D G K ___

4 D F I K N P ___

5 GF HE ID JC ___

6 HI JK LM NO PQ ___

7 KT MS OR QQ ___

8 LNQ KON JPK IQH ___

9 D B Z X V T ___

10 P J R I T H V ___

11 P H N J L L J ___

12 Q E O F L H H K ___

13 E G J N S ___

14 TS SU RW QY ___

15 D H F G H F J ___

16 R Q O L H C ___

17 TV VU XT ZS ___

18 WPC UQB SRA QSZ ___

19 K M N P Q ___

20 S H Q J P K N M ___

Unit 4. Letter Relationships

In this type of question, you are required to work out the relationship between two pairs of letters and then complete the statement using the same pattern.

For example: BD is to EF as MO is to _____

Hints

i.   Study the first letter in each of the first two pairs of letters – B and E – and work out how many moves it is from B to E. This is three moves forward in the alphabet.

ii.   Go now to the first letter of the pair in the question, that is M, and move forward three places.

Answer: P

iii.   Study the second letter in each of the first two pairs of letters, that is D and F, and work out how many moves it is from D to F. This is two moves forward in the alphabet.

iv.   Go now to the second letter of the pair in the question, that is O, and move forward two places.

Answer: Q

$$\text{BD is to EF as MO is to PQ}$$

v.   Always use an alphabet to help you.

vi.   There are sometimes three letters in each relationship. Simply follow the same hints.

Worked Examples

A B C D E F G H I J K L M N O P Q R S T U V W X Y Z

1.   AD is to CF as LO is to ____

Answer: NQ

2. QW is to NX as KD is to ____

Answer: HE

3. LQS is to NOU as TBZ is to ____

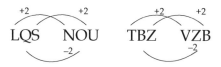

Answer: VZB

Practice Questions

Work out how the first pair of letters is connected to the second pair in order to complete the sentence. The alphabet is here to help you with these questions.

A B C D E F G H I J K L M N O P Q R S T U V W X Y Z

1   DE is to FG as MN is to (?)   _____

2   HI is to JK as PQ is to (?)   _____

3   BA is to EC as DC is to (?)   _____

4   ST is to WU as FG is to (?)   _____

5   JK is to LI as UV is to (?)   _____

6   LM is to ML as TX is to (?)   _____

7   KM is to OI as TB is to (?)   _____

8   FGH is to HIJ as PQR is to (?)   _____

9   MPQ is to LQP as JKL is to (?)   _____

10   TU is to YA as VW is to (?)   _____

11   AC is to XF as RS is to (?)   _____

12   NPQ is to MRO as FGH is to (?)   _____

13 TAF is to RCD as ATW is to (?) ───────────

14 JL is to KK as PQ is to (?) ───────────

15 GK is to EM as LP is to (?) ───────────

16 TPR is to VSV as ABD is to (?) ───────────

17 RT is to LZ as HK is to (?) ───────────

18 UVW is to TTT as FGH is to (?) ───────────

19 KMT is to JNS as RTP is to (?) ───────────

20 OBD is to RAH as KPR is to (?) ───────────

Unit 5. Codes

In this type of question, you are given a word and how it is written in code. You are then asked either to put a word into the same code or to determine what word the code represents.

There are two types of codes – simple and complex. In each of these, there is always a key as to how the code works.

Simple Code Example

In a simple code, the letters appearing in the key and the question are the same.

For example: If the code for BREAD is XPTUV, what, in the same code, does VUPT stand for?

Hints

i. Write the proper word over the code word, ensuring that the letters are directly above the letters that represent them in code.

> BREAD
> XPTUV

ii. Take good care not to confuse the code letter with the proper letter.

> BREAD
> XPTUV

It can be seen that B is represented by X and A by U and so on.
So, using the method, VUPT represents DARE.

Worked Examples

1. If XPTVD represents COAST, what is ACTS in the same code?

> COAST
> XPTVD

Answer: TXDV

2.   If QZRTV represents PRIDE, what does QRVZ stand for?

    PRIDE
    QZRTV

Answer: PIER

Complex Code Example

In a complex code, the letters appearing in the key are not the same as in the question.

For example: If ESJOL stands for DRINK, what, in the same code, represents SMILE?

Hints

i. Write the proper word over the code word, ensuring that the letters are directly above the letters that represent them in code.

    D R I N K
    E S J O L

ii. Work out the pattern which has changed the real letters into the code letters.

iii. Use an alphabet, usually given, to help you.

iv. Always work from real word to code word and write the pattern.

    D R I N K
    E S J O L
    +1 +1 +1 +1 +1

  (D to E is one move forward in the alphabet, R to S one move forward and so on.)

v. Following the same pattern, SMILE: S becomes T, M becomes N and so on.

Answer: TNJMF

vi. If working from the code word to find the real word, you retain the pattern, but reverse the operation.

For example: If given TNJMF and required to find the real word, follow the first four hints, but then go back one each time. So T back one move becomes S and N back one move becomes M, and so on.

Answer: SMILE

Worked Examples

A B C D E F G H I J K L M N O P Q R S T U V W X Y Z

1. If CARD is represented by ECTF, what is GOAL in the same code?

C	A	R	D
E	C	T	F
+2	+2	+2	+2

    Following the pattern, G going forward two moves becomes I, O becomes Q and so on.

Answer: IQCN

2. If FILM is represented by DGJK, what word does NYPR represent?

F	I	L	M
D	G	J	K
−2	−2	−2	−2

    In this case, to determine the proper word you need to reverse the pattern.

    So in NYPR, N going forward two moves gives P, Y becomes A, P becomes R and R becomes T.

Answer: PART

Practice Questions

A B C D E F G H I J K L M N O P Q R S T U V W X Y Z

The alphabet is here to help you with these questions. Work out the code for each question to find the answer. All the codes are different.

Simple Codes   **Answers**

1   If the code for AREA is BCDB, what does CDBC mean?   _____

2   If the code for LIFE is XYZQ, what does ZYXQ mean?   _____

3   If the code for MEAL is TUVB, what is the code for LAME?   _____

A B C D E F G H I J K L M N O P Q R S T U V W X Y Z

Complex Codes

4   If SCORED is UEQTGF, what is the code for VICTOR?   _____

5   If the code for EXAM is FZDQ, what does GCLP mean?   _____

6   If the code for JOKE is INJD, what does KZTFG mean?   _____

Mixed

7   If the code for NOTICE is ONUHDD, what does HQPTOC mean?   _____

8   If the code for CARE is ATVX, what does VTAX mean?   _____

9   If the code for CAKE is BYHA, what is the code for SOLD?   _____

10   If the code for MAKE is LZJD, what does AKTD mean?   _____

11   If the code for BREAK is 'CTHEP, what is the code for APPLE?   _____

12   If the code for SWORD is UUQPF, what does DPQIG mean?   _____

13   If the code for CANDLE is DZPBOB, what is the code for PACKET?   _____

14   If the code for BRUTE is XYTQZ, what is the code for TUBE?   _____

15   If the code for PIANO is TYZXU, what is the code for PAIN?   _____

16   If the code for MASTER is OYURGP, what is the code for PAIN?   _____

17   If the code for GRAPE is EPYNC, what does UGLCQ mean?   _____

18   If the code for GREAT is XYTBA, what does XBAT mean?   _____

19   If the code for DATE is EBUF, what does TPBQ mean?   _____

20   If the code for SOAP is UMCN, what is the code for DEAF?   _____

Unit 6. Combining Words

In this type of question, you are given two sets of words in brackets. In each bracket are three words. You are required to choose one word from the <u>left</u> hand bracket and, by joining it with a word in the <u>right</u> hand bracket, form a completely new word.

For example: (CAR, ROUND, BARROW)   (WHEEL, TIN, PET)

By joining the words CAR from the first bracket and PET from the second bracket, the word CARPET is formed.

Hints

i.   On occasions, by a careful study of the words in the brackets, the new word becomes immediately obvious.

ii.   If the newly created word does not become immediately obvious, then number the words in the first bracket 1,2,3 and put letters over the words in the second bracket, A,B,C. Then, mentally link the two together 1A, 1B, 1C, 2A, 2B, 2C, 3A, 3B, 3C.

iii.
For example: (COUGH¹, ICE², WATER³)   (IN^A, CREAM^B, COLD^C)

<u>1A</u>   <u>1B</u>   <u>1C</u>
COUGHIN   COUGHCREAM   COUGHCOLD

<u>2A</u>   <u>2B</u>
ICEIN   ICECREAM

iv.   Whilst mentally joining the words together very often results in the new word, this is not always the case especially when the two words, treated separately, do not sound like a new word when put together.

For example: (FEAT, PUPIL, ROUND)   (STRENGTH, HER, GOOD)

The new word is FEATHER although FEAT and HER when sounded out separately do not appear to form a new word. On the other hand, combining two words can sound correct, but are in fact incorrectly spelt. For example, LESS and SON do not form LESSON.

v.   When you have decided on a new word, make sure it is spelt properly.

vi.   Make sure that when the two words come together, they form one word and are not two words which often go together. For example: CHAIR and LEG put together do not make a correct word.

vii.   Always remember the word from the left hand bracket comes first.

Worked Examples

1.   (BUT PANT HOT)   (TRY AIR TON)

      1   2   3   A   B   C
      (BUT PANT HOT)   (TRY AIR TON)

Assume the word does not become immediately obvious.

      1A   1B   1C
      BUTTRY   BUTAIR   BUTTON

Answer: BUTTON

2.   (HAPPY BIG FAT)   (FRY LEG HER)

      1   2   3   A   B   C
      (HAPPY BIG FAT)   (FRY LEG HER)

Assume the word does not become immediately obvious.

      1A   1B   1C
      HAPPYFRY   HAPPYLEG   HAPPYHER

      3A   3B   3C
      FATFRY   FATLEG   FATHER

Answer: FATHER

Practice Questions

In the questions below choose two words, one from each bracket, that will together make one correctly spelt word. You must not change the order of the letters. The word from the bracket on the left comes first.

Underline the appropriate two words.

1   (BAG DEFER CART)   (FULL RIDGE MINT)

2   (COT STOP PLAY)   (TEN TON RIGHT)

3	(CON FLAG RAT)	(HER MENT SORE)
4	(SHRUB RIPE PLEA)	(BERRY SURE POCKET)
5	(DETER DREAD SAIL)	(AWAY MINE FULL)
6	(DEAD CLIMB FOR)	(DEN BID ATE)
7	(CLOT BANK HER)	(THING RING ROBBER)
8	(BARE REASON DRAMA)	(PLAY SKIN ABLE)
9	(QUICK POLL KID)	(ICE NAP LUTE)
10	(FORE DRUNK WITH)	(GET OUT CARD)
11	(HELP WEDDING COVE)	(FULL RING NET)
12	(PAGE CURE TOP)	(PILL ANT OVER)
13	(TINY OR HATE)	(BIT RANGE RED)
14	(RAN WEEK ALL)	(SOME TOGETHER END)
15	(MAN OLD LEAR)	(PIPE AGE OUT)
16	(PRINTED PASS TALL)	(STORY SPORT WORD)
17	(LET SUBS CAB)	(IN HIRE SIDE)
18	(MEN MESS MANE)	(ANGER AGE TALL)
19	(PROBE CLASS SO)	(UP TIME ABLY)
20	(FLAME SAFE FLEX)	(GAS GUARD ABLE)

Unit 7. Completing Words

In this type of question, you are given a sentence and a word within the sentence is incomplete. A three-letter word will complete this word. You are required to find the three-letter word.

For example: The KIDPERS demanded a large ransom.

Answer: NAP

Hints

i.   Read the sentence carefully as this gives the clue to what the incomplete word is.

ii.   Ask yourself what word would sensibly complete the sentence.

iii.   Write out the word and see which letters are missing.

iv.   If the missing letters are three in number and form a correct word, this will be the answer.

v.   It is important to appreciate the three letters can be inserted anywhere into the word.

Worked Examples

1.   The PRFUL wrestler threw his opponent to the ground.

        Having carefully read the sentence, ask how would a wrestler be described.

        An appropriate word would be POWERFUL.

        Write this word out and note that the missing three letters form a word.

Answer: OWE

2.   Always wear warm CHES in winter.

        An appropriate word in this sentence would be CLOTHES.

        Write this word out and note that the missing three letters form a word.

Answer: LOT

Practice Questions

In each of these sentences, three letters have been taken out of the word in capitals. These three letters, which make a proper word when inserted, will then make a correctly spelt word. The completed sentence must make sense.

Answer

1. The athlete walked to the STING line. _____

2. The stars TWLED in the dark sky. _____

3. The oarsman rowed up the NAR creek. _____

4. There was loud CTER in the classroom. _____

5. The pupil was COMDED for his hard work. _____

6. Egypt DEDS on the Nile for irrigation. _____

7. The FLS lit up the sky. _____

8. The motorist IGED the speed limit. _____

9. The mechanic lost his SNER. _____

10. The internet is useful for RESCH. _____

11. The puppy WPERED all night. _____

12. The traffic came to a STSTILL in the fog. _____

13. The police RETURED the escaped prisoner. _____

14. The GTH of the city's population was huge. _____

15. The COMITION between the teams was exciting. _____

16. The COMATION of hard work and brains is necessary. _____

17. It is ILAL to smuggle diamonds. _____

18. A letter INMED parents of the news. _____

19. The customers were DISISFIED with the service. _____

20. The holiday was far too EXSIVE. _____

Unit 8. Hidden Words

In this type of question, you are given a sentence. In the sentence is a hidden word. The hidden word will usually:

a)   Comprise four letters.

b)   Be formed by the end letters of one word and the beginning letters of the next word.

For example:

Every day father start<u>s ea</u>ting sweets.

In this sentence, a hidden word is found.

Answer: SEAT

Hints

i.   A slow reading of the sentence can often highlight the hidden word, especially if you concentrate on the end of one word and the beginning of the next word.

ii.   If the slow reading of the sentence fails to highlight the missing word then:

(a)   Link the last three letters of the first word with the first letter of the second word.

(b)   Link the last two letters of the first word with the first two letters of the second word.

(c)   Link the last letter of the first word with the first three letters of the second word.

Then, repeat the process with the second and third words in the sentence, then the third and fourth words and so on until a word emerges.

For example:

The teacher heard the row in the playground.

'The teacher' could be thet, hete, etea – obviously no word has emerged.

'teacher heard' could herh, erhe, rhea – obviously no word has emerged.

'heard the' could be ardt, rdth, dthe – obviously no word has emerged.

'the row' could be ther, <u>hero</u> – at which point a word has emerged.

Worked Examples

1.   The bat has been broken.

        Try the first and second words: theb   heba   ebat

        Try the second and third words: bath

Answer: BATH

2.   The toy cost under ten pounds.

        Try the first and second words: thet   heto   etoy

        Try the second and third words: toyc   oyco   ycos

        Try the third and fourth words: ostu   stun

Answer: STUN

Practice Questions

In the sentences below, a word of <u>four</u> letters is hidden at the end of one word and the beginning of the next word. Write out the hidden word.

Answers

1   The tutor senses enthusiasm.   _____

2   'I wish all of you success', the headmaster said.   _____

3   The factory was covered with black industrial grime. _____

4   Exterior angles are often obtuse angles.   _____

5   In the test all the answers had to be underlined.   _____

6   The castle disappeared as the mist descended.   _____

7   Top rodeo shows are found in Canada.   _____

8 The boy bought ten ice creams. _____

9 The booked itinerary went perfectly. _____

10 Ann was given a red umbrella. _____

11 The Roman soldier was feared. _____

12 Sweets and cakes are not healthy. _____

13 He spent exactly a month in prison. _____

14 Members of the choir must be on time. _____

15 In the questions set, each involved careful calculation. _____

16 The farmer became anxious about the fox. _____

17 The baby was ferried over the water. _____

18 Christmas television is usually boring. _____

19 The giant ogre advanced with a loud roar. _____

20 The tired players limped off. _____

Unit 9. Matching Words

In this type of question, you are given three words. The middle word, usually in a bracket, has been formed using some of the letters in the words on either side of the bracket. The letters have been selected in a particular order. You are given two words and an empty bracket and you are required to write in the bracket a word formed from letters in the words on either side of the bracket <u>in the same order</u>.

In many questions, the pattern is immediately obvious.

For example: DROWN   (DRY)   YACHT

                      DIAL   (   )   GROW

It can be seen that DRY has been formed by using the first two letters of the left hand word and the first letter of the right hand word.

Answer: DIG

Make sure your answer is a correct word – one you have used or read.

In other questions, the pattern can be more difficult to work out.

For example: PULL   (PAST)   MAST

                      BEST   (   )   CORN

Hints

i.   Number the letters in the words on either side of the completed bracket.

$\overset{1\,2\,3\,4}{\text{PULL}}$ (PAST) $\overset{5\;6\,7\,8}{\text{MAST}}$

ii.   Note the pattern of letters in the middle word.

$\overset{1\,6\;7\,8}{\text{(PAST)}}$

iii.   Number the letters in the words on either side of the empty bracket.

$\overset{1\,2\,3\,4}{\text{BEST}}$ (   ) $\overset{5\;6\,7\,8}{\text{CORN}}$

iv.   Following the same pattern, 1678, complete the missing word.

Answer: $\overset{1\,6\;7\,8}{\text{(BORN)}}$

Another degree of difficulty is added when the same letter appears in both words.

For example: BOAT (BORE) COVER
SUNG (   ) PANEL

In this instance, number the letters as above.

1 2 3 4 1 _ 9 8 5 6 78 9
BOAT (BORE) COVER

1 2 3 4 1 _ 9 8 5 6 789
SUNG (S_ L E) PANEL

At this point it is only possible to fill in three of the letters used. The final letter is determined by trying both of the possible letters to see which makes a correct word.

Answer: SALE

Worked Examples

1. SLID (IDEA) PLEA
RUSH (   ) FLED

IDEA has been formed using the last two letters of the left hand word and the last two letters of the right hand word.

Answer: SHED

2. SKIN (ISLE) LEAD
RODE (   ) UGLY

1 2 3 4 3 15 6 5 6 7 8
SKIN (ISLE) LEAD

1 2 3 4 3 1 5 6 5 6 7 8
RODE (   ) UGLY

Answer: DRUG

3. SCHOOL (LOSE) SCRAPE
ROARED (   ) FRENZY

1 2 3 4 56 6   12 7 8 9 10 11 12
SCHOOL (LOSE) SCRAPE

1 2 3 45 6 6   12 7 8 9 10 11 12
ROARED (D_ _Y) FRENZY

The possibilities include: DRFY
                              DERY
                              DRRY
                              DEFY

The only correct word is DEFY.

Answer: DEFY

Practice Questions

In the following questions the middle word has been formed from some of the letters in the words either side of the bracket. Find the missing word in the second bracket formed in the same way as the first.

Answers

1. SIGN   (SNOW)   WHOM : SOIL   (   )   PRAM   _____

2. ROPE   (POLE)   SALE : CAPS   (   )   CART   _____

3. JETS   (STAR)   CARE : BEAR   (   )   SINK   _____

4. GRANT (RAID)   IDEAS : TRIPS   (   )   PEALS   _____

5. BIRD   (BRAG)   SANG : CARE   (   )   SOUP   _____

6. GRUEL (GRAVE)   BRAVE : SPEAK   (   )   TREND   _____

7. CRUEL (CRATE)   PLATE : BLUES   (   )   TRACK   _____

8. BRING (GRAB)   BRASS : BASED   (   )   ENTER   _____

9. SCREW (SWAM)   STAMP : PEDAL   (   )   BLAND   _____

10. ACRE   (ARCH)   CHOP : CARD   (   )   ABLE   _____

11. STUNG (NICE)   PRICE : DEALS   (   )   SCONE   _____

12. SOIL   (SLOW)   WHOM : BEAR   (   )   GRAM   _____

13. RAGE   (GRAIN)   TWIN : ISLE   (   )   PETS   _____

14. SWOP   (WORM)   ROOM : SPAR   (   )   RANT   _____

15	SCRAP	(RAIL)	CLIMB	:	STABS	(	)	SELLS	_____
16	DROP	(POLE)	MALE	:	PART	(	)	SLAP	_____
17	SEND	(EDIT)	TIED	:	SCAR	(	)	MALE	_____
18	RAID	(DAMP)	PLUM	:	MEAL	(	)	SLUG	_____
19	SCORE	(RODE)	CRIED	:	STAMP	(	)	BRATS	_____
20	WARES	(WATER)	RATES	:	HOUSE	(	)	DOPED	_____

Unit 10. Word Patterns

In this type of question, you are given two pairs of words. The second word in each pair has been formed from the first word in exactly the same way. You are required to complete a third pair of words in the same way.

For example: LAME   SHAME   :   PUT   SHUT   :   PORT _____

In the above, the missing word is SHORT. The pattern throughout is removing the first letter of the first word and replacing it with SH.

Hints

i. Look at the first pair of words and work out what has happened to the first word to make it into the second word.

ii. Look at the second pair of words and check that the same pattern has been followed as in the first pair of words.

iii. If the pattern in the first and second pairs of words is the same, apply the same rule to the first word in the third pair.

iv. Always ensure that the word formed is a sensible word.

v. Common patterns will include:

   a) Removing letters

   b) Adding letters

   c) Using certain letters in a set order. For example, for GARDEN to become DEAR, the 4th, 5th, 2nd and 3rd letters have been used.

vi. In the more difficult cases, it is best to put numbers above the letters and work out a number sequence.

MARKET   RAKE   :   JACKET   CAKE   :   WALKED   _ _ _ _

Answer: LAKE

1.   SEEP SLEEP : BACK BLACK : BANK _____

Pattern: Inserting the letter L as the second letter in the word.

Answer: BLANK

2.   1 2 3 4 5 6 4 2 3 5 : 1 2 3 4 5 6 4 2 3 5 : 1 2 3 4 5 6 4 2 3 5
TALKED KALE : FORGET GORE : SACRED _ _ _ _

Answer: RACE

3.   CAR RACE : MAN NAME : BUT _ _ _ _

Pattern: The letters forming the first word in reverse order plus E.

Answer: TUBE

4.   1 2 3 4 5 6 1 4 D : 1 2 3 4 5 6 1 4 D : 1 2 3 4 5 6 7 1 4 D
PLEASE PAD : BISECT BED : CLEANER _ _ _

Pattern: The first and fourth letters have been used and the letter D added.

Answer: CAD

5.   CARE DARE : SORE TORE : MOON _ _ _ _

Pattern: The first letter of the second word is always the next letter in the alphabet after the first letter in the first word.

Answer: NOON

In the questions below there are three pairs of words. You must complete the third pair in the same way as the first two pairs.

1	BEAT	BAT	:	TWIN	TIN	: HEAT	_____
2	CREATE	CRATE	:	BLEED	BLED	: STEEP	_____
3	PART	TRAP	:	SNIP	PINS	: EDIT	_____
4	LANDS	SAND	:	BENDS	SEND	: BRING	_____

5	CRAVE	RAVES	:	STOP	TOPS	:	CRUST	_____
6	PALES	LAP	:	DOPES	POD	:	TASTE	_____
7	BRING	BIG	:	TRAIN	TAN	:	SLANT	_____
8	BOAT	BAT	:	DRUG	DUG	:	TRIP	_____
9	DRIVEL	LIVE	:	DREAMS	SEAM	:	SPRING	_____
10	SPICK	SICK	:	SLANG	SANG	:	FLIGHT	_____
11	FACTION	FRACTION	:	DEAD	DREAD	:	BEAD	_____
12	TALKS	TALL	:	FALSE	FALL	:	BELOW	_____
13	FOUR	FOR	:	COUP	COP	:	POUND	_____
14	SPEARED	PEAR	:	BLACKEN	LACK	:	CLASSED	_____
15	CRATER	RAT	:	DRUMMED	RUM	:	FANTASTIC	_____
16	SLANDER	AND	:	DESPAIR	SPA	:	DEPENDS	_____
17	REWIND	WIN	:	POLITE	LIT	:	UNKIND	_____
18	SHIP	SIP	:	FROG	FOG	:	SPIT	_____
19	BEAR	BARE	:	HEAT	HATE	:	LEAK	_____
20	JACKET	JET	:	BOMBED	BED	:	AROUND	_____
21	DAFT	FADE	:	MOCK	COME	:	CALF	_____
22	PIRATE	RIPE	:	CINDER	NICE	:	DISHES	_____
23	DISGUST	DUST	:	RUNNING	RING	:	PROVOKE	_____
24	PLUM	PUP	:	DRIP	DID	:	BRIM	_____
25	PLEASED	PAD	:	BRIEFED	BED	:	CLEANER	_____

Unit 11. Word Change

In this type of question, you are given a word which is changed into another word in either one or two stages. At each stage, one letter is changed and in so doing forms another word.

For example:

1.   J U S T

      _ _ _ _   The missing word is MUST.

      M A S T

2.   M A I D

      _ _ _ _   The missing words are SAID, then SAIL.

      _ _ _ _   Note at each stage only one letter is changed.

      S O I L

Hints

i.   Fill in the letters that appear in both words.

ii.   By trial and error, change each of the remaining letters in turn making sure that at each stage a correct word is made.

Worked Examples

1.   K I N D   K I N D   Write the I and N.

      _ _ _ _   _ I N _   a) Change either the K or D. (If we change the D to an E, this would make KINE, which is not a word.)

      F I N E   F I N E   b) Change, therefore, the K to an F to give find.

Answer: FIND

2.   S L O T   S L O T   Keep the L.

      _ _ _ _   _ L _ _   a) Change the T to a W, giving SLOW.

      _ _ _ _   _ L _ _   b) Change the S to a B, giving BLOW.

      BLEW   B L E W

Answer: SLOW and BLOW

Practice Questions

In each of the following questions, you must change the top word into the bottom word by changing one letter at each stage and in so doing make a sensible word.

1 JUST
_ _ _ _
MAST

2 TOLD
_ _ _ _
SOLE

3 PINE
_ _ _ _
SINK

4 LUMP
_ _ _ _
LIME

5 BRIM
_ _ _ _
TRIP

6 SLAP
_ _ _ _
PLAY

7 WILL
_ _ _ _
CALL

8 CASE
_ _ _ _
DASH

9 TALE
_ _ _ _
TYPE

10 WERE
_ _ _ _
TORE

11 TOLD
_ _ _ _

_ _ _ _
BELL

12 CARD
_ _ _ _

_ _ _ _
MALE

13 JUST
_ _ _ _

_ _ _ _
DUEL

14 RING
_ _ _ _

_ _ _ _
WAND

15 SLIM
_ _ _ _

_ _ _ _
PLAY

16 BURN
_ _ _ _

_ _ _ _
TORE

17 SPOT
_ _ _ _

_ _ _ _
BOAT

18 SOME
_ _ _ _

_ _ _ _
HOLD

19 CALL
_ _ _ _

_ _ _ _
BARE

20 PLAY
_ _ _ _

_ _ _ _
TRAP

Unit 12. Word Order

In this type of question, you are given a sentence in which two words are in the wrong place. You are required to choose the two words which need to change position in order for the sentence to make complete sense.

For example: The wind sailed against the yacht.

In the example, by changing the position of wind and yacht, the sentence now makes sense.

The yacht sailed against the wind.

Answer: wind and yacht

Hints

i.   Read slowly and try to understand what the sentence is about. In the majority of questions, the full meaning will become clear and you will find the answer quite easily.

ii.   If you cannot immediately spot which are the two words, then remember that one noun in the sentence will often change places with another noun, an adjective with an adjective and so on.

Worked Examples

1.   The noisy teacher silenced the strict class.

Answer: noisy and strict

In this case, two adjectives have changed position.

2.   The crowd scored when the footballer roared.

Answer: scored and roared

In this case, two verbs have changed position.

3.   The choir sang softly while the organ played loudly.

Answer: softly and loudly

In this case, two adverbs have changed position.

Practice Questions

In the following questions, change the position of two words in order for the sentence to make sense.

1 At the end of the postbox was a busy street.

2 It was sunny, but a very winter morning.

3 The injured nurse was helping the kind lady.

4 The boy was escaping to see the frightened bank robber.

5 The short dog had a young, black coat.

6 She liked living at the house in the sea.

7 In a huge storm, the wild oak tree fell down.

8 The girl won a competition and entered first prize.

9 They set down off a small country lane.

10 The fruit in the dish came from the apple market.

11 The last victory goal gave minute.

12 The plane fog delayed by was.

13 After a hard draw it ended in a game.

14 A history showed survey to be very popular.

15 The up of lightning lit flash the sky.

16 The postman dog attacked the angry.

17 The silenced snowfall heavy the traffic.

18 The beach was holiday with happy crowded makers.

19 An isosceles equal has two triangle sides.

20 The children laughed at clown circus the.

Unit 13. Vocabulary Questions 1: Common Word

In this type of question, you are given two pairs of words. You are also given a list of words, usually five, and from the list you are required to select one word that will go with both sets of words.

For example: (fatigue weary)   (banner emblem)
streamer tire flag pennant diminish

Hints

i.   Carefully look at the two sets of words and the list of possible answers.

ii.   Select <u>one</u> set of words, always choosing the set that are the easiest for you to understand. In the above, (banner emblem).

iii.   Study the answers and eliminate words that you know do not have the same meaning as banner and emblem, retaining any words you are unsure of. Remember, nouns go with nouns, verbs with verbs and so on.

iv.   Using the above process, we could eliminate tire and diminish.

v.   Now look at the second set of words. There are now only three possible answers. Decide which goes best with the words in the other set.

Answer: flag

Worked Examples

1.   (rigid secure)   (hunger starve)
hard   fixed   fast   famine   speed

Following the hints:

a)   The set of chosen words is hunger and starve.

b)   Applying those words to the list of possible answers, we could eliminate hard, fixed and speed.

c)   Now look at the second set. Of the two remaining words – fast and famine – which goes best with rigid and secure?

Answer: fast

2.   (drawing   design)   (plot   conspire)
       architect   sketch   intrigue   strategy   scheme

Following the hints:

a)   The set of chosen words is drawing and design.

b)   Applying those words to the list of possible answers, we could eliminate architect, intrigue and strategy.

c)   Now look at the second set. Of the two remaining words – sketch and scheme – which goes best with plot and conspire?

Answer: scheme

Practice Questions

In the following questions, there are two sets of words in brackets. You must find the word from the list of answer choices that will go equally well with both pairs of words.

Now try these:

1   (cancel   eliminate)   (overthrow   destroy)
      postpone   reduce   abolish   defeat   conquer

2   (abandon   leave)   (waste   barren)
      abdicate   yield   fertile   depart   desert

3   (portion   role)   (segment   fragment)
      linger   bulk   quantity   unit   part

4   (edge   margin)   (fringe   perimeter)
      cutting   diameter   border   space   distance

5   (dispute   quarrel)   (contrast   dissimilarity)
      agree   coincide   difference   sharp   divide

6   (like   matched)   (balanced   symmetrical)
      varied   diverse   equation   scale   equal

7   (skirmish   contest)   (feud   combat)
      victory   aggressor   championship   fight   armed

8   (pin   cut)   (staple   trim)
      fix   nick   secure   clip   clamp

9 (abandon leave)   (cease stop)
desert   evacuate   quite   discard   withdraw

10 (performance pretend)   (feat behave)
entertain   show   action   act   conduct

11 (withdraw extract)   (erase eradicate)
defeat   copy   remove   surrender   mistake

12 (miniature diminutive)   (microscopic negligible)
unimportant   minute   reduced   trivial   midget

13 (delicate flimsy)   (frail feeble)
sculptor   rare   fragile   expensive   light

14 (hide cover)   (disguise cloak)
search   spy   secret   pretend   conceal

15 (distinct obvious)   (transparent understandable)
explanation   answer   clear   outlined   separate

16 (alteration transformation)   (alter modify)
conform   repair   improve   adapt   change

17 (arrange folder)   (line list)
paper   stationery   order   logical   file

18 (reluctant undecided)   (doubtful uncertain)
lazy   resolute   hesitant   steadfast   staunch

19 (routine mannerism)   (dress tendency)
programme   style   method   habit   characteristic

20 (enormous gigantic)   (considerable significant)
expansive   muscular   magnified   great   heavy

Unit 14. Vocabulary Questions 2: Opposites

In this type of question, you are given two sets of words. Each set has three words and you are required to select two words – one word from each set – that are <u>most</u> opposite in meaning.

For example: (accurate true distance) (correct inexact near)

Answer: accurate and inexact

As in all vocabulary questions, a great deal depends on acquired vocabulary, but the following hints will serve to help.

Hints

i.   Always read the instructions very carefully, making certain you provide the answer required – in this case, words which are opposite.

ii.   Read all the words slowly.

iii.   Remember you are required to find the two words which are most opposite, not vaguely opposite.

iv.   Always match a noun with a noun, a verb with a verb and so on.

v.   If the answer is not immediately obvious, then match the first word (or a word you know the meaning of) in the left hand bracket with each of the words in the right hand bracket and continue this with the second and third word until you have found the best match.

Worked Example

In the following question, select one word from each bracket. Be sure to choose the two words that are most opposite in meaning.

(activity eager energetic)   (lively sleep listless)

As the answer is not immediately obvious after reading the instructions and the two sets of words, select the first word in the left hand bracket and match it to each of the words in the right hand bracket.

By applying the third word on the left (energetic) and matching it to each of the words in the right hand bracket, the answer becomes evident.

Answer: energetic and listless

Note: If the hints had not been followed, then activity and listless could have been selected. (One is a noun and the other an adjective.)

Practice Questions

In the following questions underline two words, one from each bracket, that are the most opposite in meaning.

1 (generous scarce plenty) (extra sparse selfish)

2 (rigid relaxation mature) (dullness flexible retirement)

3 (narrow balanced slanted) (scale angle lopsided)

4 (conclusion commencement expire) (termination breathe prevent)

5 (amazing minute immense) (time diminutive spectacular)

6 (obscure clear radiant) (shine distinct tactless)

7 (satisfied pretend irritated) (false contented masked)

8 (accurate true compare) (factual different inexact)

9 (average typical unique) (rare common usual)

10 (casual determined weak) (clumsiness effort careful)

11 (military heroism amble) (cowardice stroll army)

12 (resume help pause) (maintain proceed support)

13 (hinder hasten encourage) (suspend detach assist)

14 (aid drawback improve) (benefit safe harmless)

15 (learned ignorant muddle) (confusion awareness educated)

16 (blameless responsible wrong) (involved guilty damaged)

17 (restricted extended confined) (limited brief shortened)

18 (roar quiet piercing) (noisy thunder tumultuous)

19 (destroy division sector) (part create foundation)

20 (rescue intact cargo) (damaged save recover)

Unit 15. Vocabulary Questions 3: Words Closest in Meaning

In this type of question, you are given two sets of words. Each set has three words and you are required to select two words – one word from each set – that are <u>closest</u> in meaning.

For example: (achieve actual adjust) (attain fictional leave)

Answer: achieve and attain

As in all vocabulary questions, a great deal depends on acquired vocabulary, but the following hints will serve to help.

Hints

i. Always read the instructions very carefully, making certain you provide the answer required – in this case, words which mean the same.

ii. Read all the words slowly.

iii. Remember you are required to find the two words which are closest in meaning and not vaguely similar.

iv. Remember you are choosing two words which mean the same, not simply words which often link to each other.

For example: fish and chips

v. Always match a noun with a noun, a verb with a verb and so on.

vi. If the answer is not immediately obvious, then match the first word (or a word you know the meaning of) in the left hand bracket with each of the words in the right hand bracket and continue this with the second and third word until you have found the best match.

vii. You can often check by substituting the two words chosen in the same sentence.

Worked Example

In the following question, select one word from each bracket. Be sure to pick the words which are closest in meaning.

(irritated satisfied pretence)   (contented false masked)

As the answer is not immediately obvious after reading the instructions and the two sets of words, select the first word in the left hand bracket and match to each of the words in the right hand bracket, then try the second word in the left hand bracket, and so on.

By applying the second word on the left (satisfied) and matching it to each of the words in the right hand bracket, the answer becomes evident.

Answer: satisfied and contented

Note: If the method had not been followed then pretence and false could easily have been selected.   (One is a noun and one is an adjective.)

Practice Questions

In the following questions, underline the two words – one from each bracket – that are closest in meaning.

1 (access accident abundant)   (tragedy plentiful emergency)

2 (adore admire advise)   (respect despise encourage)

3 (kind pain loyalty)   (comfort caring betrayal)

4 (amaze ample alter)   (anticipate change insufficient)

5 (anger answer anxious)   (query assured wrath)

6 (cause cease catastrophe)   (prevent misfortune start)

7 (fuss comfort praise)   (console condense award)

8 (preserve connect destroy)   (fasten detain demolish)

9 (meagre magnify increase)   (reduce scanty discourage)

10 (area edge centre)   (square distance rim)

11 (retain embrace eject)   (routine expel confront)

12 (envy erode error)   (strengthen accuracy resentment)

13 (flourish shift ignore)   (decline plunder thrive)

14 (adviser obstruct guard)   (endanger defend threaten)

15 (image show plan)   (route copy parade)

16 (exhaustion fair confirm)   (just prejudice unreasonable)

17 (legal lack retain)   (adequacy sufficiency scarcity)

18 (glisten intensify darkness)   (shadow glow unburden)

19 (plunge vague incline)   (swerve height unclear)

20 (difficulty deceive disclose)   (neglect divulge easy)

Unit 16. Vocabulary Questions 4: Odd One Out

In this type of question, you are given a list of words. There are often five words and you are asked to select two which do not belong with the other three.

For example: nervous   tense   constant   apprehensive   tranquil

Answer: constant and tranquil

As in all vocabulary questions, a great deal depends on acquired vocabulary, but the following hints will serve to help.

Hints

i.   Always read the instructions very carefully, making certain you provide the answer required. For example, are two words or is one word to be chosen? In the worked examples and the practice questions below, two words are needed to be correct.

ii.   Read each of the words slowly.

iii.   It is very often easier to find three words with the same meaning, thus leaving you with the two "odd ones".

iv.   Those three words will all be the same part of speech. That is, all nouns, all adjectives and so on.

Worked Examples

1.   In the following question which two words do not belong?

scarcity   abundance   deficiency   lack   excess

Having read the instructions and then the list of words, use your knowledge of vocabulary and try to select three words which have the same meaning. In this case, scarcity, deficiency and lack. This leaves the "odd ones".

Answer: abundance and excess

2.   In the following question which two words do not belong?

despise   loathe   like   hate   esteem

Reading the instructions and list of words, the three words with the same meaning are despise, loathe and hate.

Answer: like and esteem

Practice Questions

In the following lists of words there are two words that do not belong to the rest. Underline each of the words.

1. aid obstruct support serve hinder

2. partially completely altogether entirely selection

3. reply response challenge acknowledgement inquiry

4. capture release ignored seize arrest

5. authorise prohibit sanction ban disallow

6. arrogant timid conceited reserved modest

7. mystify muddle advise bewilder educate

8. spacious restricted ample extensive confined

9. fascinate enthral repel enchant antagonise

10. turmoil routine confusion chaos order

11. surrender conquest triumph victory submission

12. scarce abundance plentiful meagre ample

13. delay impede hasten obstruct speed

14. ravine hill dune cliff gorge

15. exalt humiliate embarrass mortify honour

16. instruct educate deceive coach neglect

17. isolate segregate continue unite separate

18. prejudiced fair devious just impartial

19. annoy insult captivate conciliate irritate

20. replica imitation prototype original copy

Unit 17. Sentence Connections

In this type of question, there is a sentence which has two sets of words inside brackets. Each bracket contains three words. You are required to select one word from each bracket which best completes the sentence.

For example: Four is to (eight, group, fourth) as three is to (twelve, third, number)

Answer: fourth and third

Hints

i.   Read the sentence slowly and carefully.

ii.   Having read the sentence think of a possible connection between the two parts of the sentence, usually joined by the word 'as'.

iii.   Now test that you have linked both parts of the sentence in an identical way.

Example: Remember is to (memory, birthday, forget) as enter is to (exit, turnstile, competition).

Answer: forget and exit

These have been chosen because forget is the opposite of remember and, therefore, we have to choose the opposite of enter in order to link both parts of the sentence in an identical way.

Worked Examples

1.   Barge is to (transport, boat, canal) as lorry is to (load, petrol, motorway).

Answer: canal and motorway

        These have been chosen because a barge travels on a canal and a lorry travels on a motorway. Note the identical link.

2.   Fair is to (games, fun, fare) as piece is to (part, peace, slice)

Answer: fare and peace

        These have been chosen because fair and fare sound the same but are spelt differently; therefore, the identical link to piece is peace.

Practice Questions

In each of the following questions, there is the same connection between the word outside each set of brackets and one word inside each set of brackets. Underline the two words, one in each bracket.

1. Soldier is to (weapon, uniform, army) as sailor is to (sea, navy, ship).

2. Tree is to (trunk, wood, forest) as flower is to (petal, vase, stem).

3. Cricket is to (pitch, bat, run) as tennis is to (match, serve, racquet).

4. Copper is to (cutlery, gold, coin) as paper is to (present, note, school).

5. Leopard is to (cat, wild, spot) as tiger is to (zoo, stripe, fierce).

6. Tortoise is to (slow, shell, hibernate) as cheetah is to (shrub, fast, speed).

7. Tap is to (water, trap, rhythm) as fill is to (jug, full, frill).

8. Four is to (eight, group, quartet) as three is to (twelve, trio, number).

9. Laugh is to (happy, joke, clown) as cry is to (handkerchief, sad, tears).

10. Coffee is to (drink, bean, mug) as tea is to (kettle, supper, leaf).

11. Enemy is to (foe, war, battle) as ally is to (victory, friend, treaty).

12. Ecstatic is to (heaven, applause, delighted) as wretched is to (poor, miserable, pauper).

13. Triangle is to (line, three, rectangle) as square is to (angle, four, shape).

14. Doctor is to (patient, surgery, medicine) as lawyer is to (judge, punish, court).

15. Angry is to (cross, line, oar) as safe is to (money, driver, secure).

16. Wave is to (whale, leave, ocean) as current is to (cake, river, fish).

17. Net is to (goal, football, fish) as trap is to (mouse, door, cellar).

18. Sole is to (soul, shoe, one) as sale is to (bargain, sail, reduction).

19. Mine is to (dig, possess, gold) as well is to (health, oil, pipe).

20. Glider is to (noise, loud, aircraft) as liner is to (harbour, ships, ocean).

Unit 18. Number Series

In this type of question, you are given a series of numbers and are required to find the next number, or numbers, in the series.

Example: 1   5   9   13   __

Hints

i.   Look to see if the numbers are ascending or descending in reasonably small intervals.

Write in the gap between the numbers and you will usually find a pattern. Simply continue the pattern.

$$\overset{+4}{1}\ \ \overset{+4}{5}\ \ \overset{+4}{9}\ \ \overset{+4}{13}\ \ \underline{17}$$
∧   ∧   ∧   ∧

$$\overset{-2}{31}\ \ \overset{-2}{29}\ \ \overset{-2}{27}\ \ \overset{-2}{25}\ \ \underline{23}$$
∧   ∧   ∧   ∧

ii.   Look to see if the numbers are ascending or descending at larger intervals. In this case, the numbers are probably being multiplied or divided by the same number, <u>but</u> not always.

2   4   8   16   __

$$\overset{×2}{2}\ \ \overset{×2}{4}\ \ \overset{×2}{8}\ \ \overset{×2}{16}\ \ \underline{32}$$
∧   ∧   ∧   ∧

80   40   20   10   __

$$\overset{÷2}{80}\ \ \overset{÷2}{40}\ \ \overset{÷2}{20}\ \ \overset{÷2}{10}\ \ \underline{5}$$
∧   ∧   ∧   ∧

2   2   4   12   48   __

$$\overset{×1}{2}\ \ \overset{×2}{2}\ \ \overset{×3}{4}\ \ \overset{×4}{12}\ \ \overset{×5}{48}\ \ \underline{240}$$
∧   ∧   ∧   ∧   ∧

iii.   If the numbers in the series are going up and down alternately then the series is probably what might be called a 'jumper'.

2   3   4   7   6   11   8   __   __

Once you have realised it's a jumper, start at the first number and jump to the third, the fifth and so on, following the method above. Then return to the second and jump to the fourth and so on.

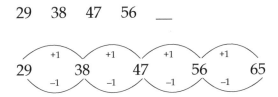

Note: The answer is <u>15</u> <u>10</u>, not <u>10</u> <u>15</u>.

If only one number is required, make sure you follow the correct series to achieve the right answer.

iv.   Often in the series there are two numbers. These can be solved as in Hint i, particularly when the numbers are small. It can, however, be regarded as two separate series. In such instances, regard it as two separate series: the first number in each, then the second number in each.

$$29 \quad 38 \quad 47 \quad 56 \quad \_\_$$

$$\overset{+1}{29} \quad \underset{-1}{\quad} \overset{+1}{38} \quad \underset{-1}{\quad} \overset{+1}{47} \quad \underset{-1}{\quad} \overset{+1}{56} \quad \underset{-1}{\quad} 65$$

Occasionally in the series there are three numbers.

$$391 \quad 483 \quad 575 \quad \underline{667}$$

In such cases there are three separate series.

v.   A small number of series do not conform to the above.

a)   2 3 5 7 11 13 <u>17</u> (all prime numbers)

b)   4 9 16 25 <u>36</u> (all square numbers)

c)   2 3 5 8 <u>13</u> (two numbers added together to form a third number)

vi.   Remember to do written calculations whenever necessary.

Worked Examples

1.   5   10   16   23   __

In this case the numbers are going up steadily. Therefore, write in the gaps.

$$\overset{+5}{5} \quad \overset{+6}{10} \quad \overset{+7}{16} \quad \overset{+8}{23} \quad \underline{31}$$

2.   3   6   12   24   __

The numbers are increasing rapidly. Therefore, try multiplying.

$\overset{\times 2}{3}$ $\overset{\times 2}{6}$ $\overset{\times 2}{12}$ $\overset{\times 2}{24}$ $\underline{48}$

3.   1   2   3   5   8   __

Since there is no regular pattern in the gaps and it is not a jumper, try adding two numbers to make the third.

1   2   3   5   8 $\underline{13}$
    1+2 = 3   2+3 = 5   3+5 = 8   5+8 = 13

4.   20   19   17   18   14   17   11   __

As the numbers are going down and then up, this is a jumper. Check whether the missing number belongs to the series beginning with the first number or the second number.

20   19   17   18   14   17   11 $\underline{16}$
          −1   −1   −1

5.   34   55   76   __

As this is a double series, go from the first number to the first number and then repeat the process with the second numbers.

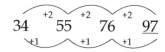

          +2   +2   +2
34   55   76 $\underline{97}$
   +1   +1   +1

Practice Questions

In these questions you need to find the number that will continue the series in the most sensible way.

1   6   10   14   18   ____

2   31   29   27   25   ____

3   6   9   13   18   24   ____

4   41   39   36   32   27   ____

5   3   6   12   24   48   ____

6	4	8	24	96	480	___

7	648	216	72	24	___

8	432	216	72	36	12	___

9	4	5	8	6	12	7	16	___

10	1	5	4	10	7	15	10	___

11	1	2	1	4	2	6	6	8	___

12	3	2	6	5	10	8	15	11	___

13	39	38	37	33	34	28	30	23	___

14	2	5	7	12	19	31	___

15	1	9	25	49	81	___

16	972	763	554	345	___

17	17	18	15	16	12	14	8	12	___

18	198	377	556	735	___

19	4	9	7	12	10	15	13	___

20	3	5	12	11	48	18	192	26	___

Unit 19. Number Substitution

In this type of question, letters are given a number value. You are required to carry out a mathematical operation using these values.

For example: When A = 8   B = 5   C = 10   D = 4

Then (A × B) ÷ C becomes (8 × 5) ÷ 10 = 4 <u>or</u> D

Hints

i.   Write above each letter its number value.

ii.   Work out the answer using the rules of mathematics, remembering:

(a)   When A = 6   3A = 18 (that is 3 × A) and <u>not</u> 36

(b)   When there are brackets, first work out the value of the bracket.

(c)   A number in front of a bracket means that, after working out the sum inside the bracket, you multiply the answer by that number.

Example: 3(8 + 6) becomes 3 × 14 = 42

(d)   When one letter is placed over another, for example $\frac{C}{B}$, this means the top letter value is divided by the bottom letter value.

Example: When C = 12 and B = 3, then $\frac{C}{B}$ is $\frac{12}{3} = 4$

(e)   When two letters appear together, for example DC, this means the two number values are multiplied.

Example: If D equals 5 and C equals 3, the answer is 15.

(f)   Given, for example, 12 − 15 + 5, it is best, if unsure about negative numbers, to add first before doing the subtraction.

So, 12 + 5 is 17 and then minus 15 gives the answer 2.

Worked Examples

When A = 5   B = 6   C = 7 and D = 3, what is the value of the following? Answer as a letter.

1. $(3A + B) \div C$

Following the hints, write the values above the letters.

$(3\overset{5}{A} + \overset{6}{B}) \div \overset{7}{C}$

Apply the mathematical rules.

Work out the bracket first.

3A means 3 × 5 = 15 + 6 = 21

Then 21 ÷ 7 = 3

Answer: D

2. $\dfrac{7A}{C}$

Write the values above the letters.

$\dfrac{7\overset{5}{A}}{\overset{7}{C}}$

Apply the rules.

7A means 7 × 5 = 35

Then 35 ÷ 7 = 5

Answer: A

3. $A - B + C$

Write the values above the letters.

$\overset{5}{A} \overset{-}{} \overset{6}{B} \overset{+}{} \overset{7}{C}$

Using the hint, add 5 + 7 first which equals 12 and then take 6, giving the answer 6.

Answer: B

Practice Questions

1 In the following code A = 8   B = 6   C = 4   D = 2

Work out the following, in each case giving your answer as a letter.

i.   A × B ÷ (A + C)

ii.   2A – 2B

iii. 5A – (4B + 3C)

iv.   3A ÷ B

2 In the following code A = 2   B = 4   C = 6   D = 8

Work out the following, in each case giving your answer as a letter.

i.   B + A

ii. $\dfrac{D}{A}$

iii. C – D + B

iv.   A (D – C)

3 In the following code A = 6   B = 12   C = 4   D = 3

Work out the following:

i.   5B ÷ (A + C) Give your answer as a letter.

ii.   2B ÷ C Give your answer as a letter.

iii. 4B ÷ CD Give your answer as a letter.

iv. $\dfrac{B}{C}$ Give your answer as a letter.

4 A = 4   B = 6   C = 2   D = 8   E = 10

i.   A + B – C

ii.   DC – B

iii. E – D + C

iv. $C\left[\dfrac{D}{A}\right]$

5 A = 6 B = 7 C = 4 D = 9 E = 2

    i.   2A – B + C

    ii   (A ÷ E) + (B – C)

    iii.   C – D + B

    iv.   E (B – C)

6 A = 5 B = 3 C = 1 D = 0 E = 4

    i.   A + B – C – D – E

    ii.   B × E × D

    iii.   B – E + A

    iv.   EB – (A + B + E)

Unit 20. Number Relationships

In this type of question, you are given three groups of numbers. Each group comprises a number in a bracket and numbers on either side of the bracket.

For example: 3 (7) 4

The number inside the bracket is a result of a mathematical operation involving the two numbers either side of the bracket. In this case, 3 and 4 have been added to give 7.

The same operation is repeated in the next two groups of numbers.

Thus,   3 (7) 4   8 (17) 9   6 (   ) 8

You are required to find the missing number in the third group.

Answer: 14 (6+8).

Hints

i.   Remember the <u>same</u> pattern has to be applied to all three groups.

ii.   Look at the number in the middle. If it is larger than the two numbers on the outside, then try adding or multiplying the two numbers.

Example: 9 (45) 5   6 (54) 9   11 (66) 6

        In this case the two outside numbers have been multiplied.

iii.   Similarly, if the number in the middle is smaller try subtracting or dividing the two outside numbers.

Example: 24 (17) 7   36 (9) 27   18 (14) 4

        In this case the two outside numbers have been subtracted.

iv.   Often, after completing one process, you then have to do a second process. Look at your first answer and determine what needs to be done to get the middle number.

Example: 6 (15) 5   12 (36) 6   14 (28) 4

        In this case, either multiply the two numbers on the outside and then divide your answer by two or first halve the first number and then multiply by the second number.

Example: 3 (15) 4   5 (33) 6   4 (31) 7

In this case, the two numbers on the outside have been multiplied together and 3 added to that number.

Worked Examples

1.   7 (15) 8   9 (12) 3   6 ( ) 11

Look at the number in the middle. As it is larger, try adding or multiplying. In this case adding the two numbers will give you the answer.

Answer: 17

2.   12 (11) 5   44 (25) 3   60 ( ) 8

As the number in the middle is smaller, try subtracting or dividing. Since neither operation results in the middle number, something may have been done first, to one or both of the outside numbers. In this case, the first is halved before adding the second number to give the middle number.

Answer: 38

Practice Questions

In the following questions the numbers in each group are related in the same way. You must find the missing number in the third group.

1	5 (22) 17	9 (23) 14	6 ( ) 17
2	29 (11) 18	31 (17) 14	43 ( ) 19
3	6 (15) 3	9 (26) 8	13 ( ) 6
4	8 (48) 6	7 (56) 8	9 ( ) 11
5	45 (3) 15	48 (3) 16	66 ( ) 22
6	20 (24) 8	36 (42) 12	64 ( ) 24
7	6 (36) 2	7 (63) 3	5 ( ) 4
8	5 (21) 8	8 (28) 10	20 ( ) 8

9	18 (45) 5	34 (51) 3	42 ( ) 5
10	7 (48) 7	8 (47) 6	9 ( ) 6
11	8 (66) 14	7 (51) 10	10 ( ) 6
12	16 (3) 4	36 (8) 4	18 ( ) 6
13	21 (32) 10	19 (18) 20	9 ( ) 8
14	6 (47) 7	8 (37) 4	10 ( ) 3
15	17 (6) 13	41 (9) 4	11 ( ) 9
16	30 (12) 17	27 (7) 19	18 ( ) 6
17	18 (6) 6	24 (6) 8	30 ( ) 6
18	24 (6) 6	37 (10) 13	19 ( ) 31
19	8 (27) 11	6 (20) 8	8 ( ) 12
20	37 (150) 13	6 (27) 3	11 ( ) 7

Unit 21. Matching Words and Symbols

In this type of question, you are usually given a set of words and a set of symbols. You are then required to match each word with the correct symbols.

For example: MEAT   TEAM   MATE   MEET

         (i)   x ! ? +

         (ii)   ? + ! x

         (iii)   x + + ?

         (iv)   x + ! ?

On occasion the number of words might exceed the sets of symbols. This is simply to make the question more difficult.

Hints

i.   Study the words and symbols for clues.

      (a)   Do two or three words start with the same letter?

      (b)   Do two or three words end with the same letter?

      (c)   Does any word contain the same letter more than once?

      (d)   Does any word have two of the same letter together?

ii.   By using the above you will discover a symbol representing a specific letter.

iii.   Once you are certain, write the letter above the same symbol in all the words.

Worked Example

       RATE   TEAR   REAR   TREE

        (i)   + x ? +

        (ii)   + ? @ x

        (iii)   @ + x x

        (iv)   @ x ? +

Study the pattern of the letters in the words and the pattern of the symbols.

One word – TREE – has two of the same letter together. By studying the pattern of the symbols, x must stand for E. Write E above every x.

$$+ \overset{E}{x} \ ? \ +$$

$$+ \ ? \ @ \ \overset{E}{x}$$

$$@ + \overset{E}{x} \ \overset{E}{x}$$

$$@ \ \overset{E}{x} \ ? \ +$$

Following from this, T is represented by @ and R is represented by +.

By following the method of writing the letter above the symbol, the words become apparent.

It is essential not to guess. For example, + could be guessed as representing the letter T or the @ could be taken to be R.

Practice Questions

In each of the following sentences there are sets of words and sets of symbols. Each set of symbols represents one of the words. Match the correct word for each set of symbols.

1   BLAME   TABLE   LABEL   BLADE   BLEED

i.   +   X   ?   !   @   i.   _____

ii.   +   X   @   @   ÷   ii.   _____

iii.   +   X   ?   ÷   @   iii.   _____

iv.   X   ?   +   @   X   iv.   _____

2   LIVE   EVIL   VEIN   VILE   VEIL

i.   X   +   @   !   i.   _____

ii.   !   @   +   X   ii.   _____

iii.   @   +   X   !   iii.   _____

iv.   @   !   +   X   iv.   _____

3 PEAL   PEAR   LEAP   PALE

i.   X   !   @   +   i.   ——————————

ii.   X   @   +   !   ii. ——————————

iii. +   !   @   X   iii. ——————————

4 DEER   REAR   READ   AREA

i.   +   −   X   ?   i.   ——————————

ii.   +   −   X   +   ii. ——————————

iii. X   +   −   X   iii. ——————————

5 RADAR   TRADE   DATED   DREAD   DARED

i.   X   ÷   @   !   X   i.   ——————————

ii.   ÷   !   X   !   ÷   ii. ——————————

iii. X   !   ÷   @   X   iii. ——————————

iv.   X   !   ?   @   X   iv. ——————————

6 BARED   DREAD   DARED   BRAID   BREED

i.   ?   !   @   ÷   ?   i.   ——————————

ii.   ?   @   ÷   !   ?   ii. ——————————

iii. X   @   ÷   ÷   ?   iii. ——————————

iv.   X   !   @   ÷   ?   iv. ——————————

7 APPLE   EAGLE   PALED   PLEAD

i.   ?   @   =   X   !   i.   ——————————

ii.   ?   X   @   =   !   ii. ——————————

iii. X   ?   ?   @   =   iii. ——————————

8 MILES   SINGS   ISLES   SLIME

i.   X   +   @   ÷   !   i.   ——————————

ii.   ÷   @   +   !   X   ii. ——————————

iii. @   X   +   !   X   iii. ——————————

Unit 22. Interpretation of Data

In this type of question, you are given information and required to answer a number of questions based on the information.

For example:

Tom, Bill, Fred and Jack were asked which lessons they enjoyed. Tom, Fred and Jack enjoy history. Bill and Fred enjoy geography. Bill and Jack enjoy art. All except Fred enjoy music.

1.   Who enjoys just geography, music and art?

2.   Who enjoys just history and geography?

3.   Who enjoys just history, music and art?

Hints

i.   Draw a grid.

	History	Geography	Art	Music
Tom				
Bill				
Fred				
Jack				

It is best to abbreviate in a sensible way.

ii.   On the grid, put in the information contained in the question.

	H	G	A	M
T	✓	x	x	✓
B	x	✓	✓	✓
F	✓	✓	x	x
J	✓	x	✓	✓

iii. Use the grid to answer the questions.

   1. Bill just enjoys geography, music and art.

   2. Fred just enjoys history and geography.

   3. Jack just enjoys history, music and art.

Whilst constructing a grid might be considered a possible waste of time, this is not the case. Once the grid is completed the questions are quickly and accurately answered.

Worked Example

Five holiday resorts were studied for the facilities they offered to visitors. A and D possess a pier. All but C and E have a fairground. Only A does not have a golf course and only B and C do not have a marina.

1. Which resort has a pier, fairground, golf course and marina?

2. Which resort has only a golf course and marina?

3. Which resort only has a golf course?

	P	F	G	M
A	✓	✓	x	✓
B	x	✓	✓	x
C	x	x	✓	x
D	✓	✓	✓	✓
E	x	x	✓	✓

1. Resort D has a pier, fairground, golf course and marina.

2. Resort E has only a golf course and marina.

3. Resort C has just a golf course.

Practice Questions

1 Five children, Alan, Bernard, Colin, David and Edward, were asked what countries they had visited. All but Bernard have been to Spain. Colin and Edward have

been to Italy. Colin and David have visited France. All but David have been to the USA.

a) Who had only visited the USA?

b) Who had visited four countries?

c) Who had visited only Spain and the USA?

d) Who had visited only Spain and France?

2 Tom, Harry, Fred and Alan were asked whether they liked coffee, tea, milk and chocolate. Harry was the only one who disliked chocolate. Only Fred and Alan liked tea. All liked coffee except Harry, and only Tom and Fred did not like milk.

a) What drinks were enjoyed by Tom?

b) How many drinks did Harry enjoy?

c) What drink was not enjoyed by Fred?

3 5 men, A, B, C, D and E, want to get together to play darts.

A can play on Tuesdays and Fridays.

B cannot play on Tuesdays, Thursdays or Saturdays.

C can play only on Mondays, Wednesdays and Fridays.

D cannot play on Mondays and Wednesdays.

E cannot play on Thursdays.

Sundays are not included.

a) On which day can they all play?

b) Who can play on the greatest number of days?

c) On which day can the fewest play?

d) On which day can only two players play?

e) On what days can A and D play together?

f) On what days, except Friday, can D and E play together?

4 A, B, C, D and E are men of different nationalities.

A, C and E speak English.

B and D speak German.

A and D speak French.

B and E speak Spanish.

C speaks Russian.

    a)   Who can speak English and Spanish?

    b)   Who can speak English and French?

    c)   Who can speak German and French?

5 Five children were asked what flavours of ice cream they liked from a choice of vanilla, strawberry, chocolate, raspberry and mint. Alan said he liked vanilla, strawberry and mint. Bill said he did not like vanilla and chocolate. All but one liked mint. David said he liked vanilla, strawberry and chocolate. Colin only liked one flavour. Erica said she did not like chocolate and raspberry.

    a)   Who had the same taste as Alan?

    b)   Who liked strawberry, raspberry and mint?

    c)   Which flavour does Colin enjoy?

    d)   How many liked raspberry?

    e)   How many did not like strawberry?

6 Five children were asked what board games they played. Ann plays draughts, ludo and Monopoly. Bill plays chess, ludo and Scrabble. All play Monopoly except Bill. David plays all games except ludo. Elizabeth plays draughts, ludo and Monopoly. Colin does not play draughts, ludo or chess.

    a)   What game could Bill and Elizabeth play together?

    b)   Who likes the same games as Elizabeth?

    c)   What game can Bill, Colin and David play together?

    d)   How many play just three games?

    e)   Who, together with Elizabeth, does not play Scrabble?

Answers to Practice Questions

1. Transferring Letters

1.	DROP	MOAN
2.	HORSE	AVENUE
3.	PAIN	TEAR
4.	ONE	NEITHER
5.	FAME	SLIGHT
6.	LIMB	SCENT
7.	CAP	SLIP
8.	TIP	BIRD
9.	CAT	BOAT
10.	SENT	CARE
11.	PANT	CAMEL
12.	BACK	BELT
13.	CAR	SHED
14.	CASE	POET
15.	WING	GRASP
16.	PAD	PAIL
17.	MAY	SAND
18.	TANK	SHORE
19.	FOG	FLEW
20.	RIG	TOWN

2. Missing Letters

1.	D
2.	N
3.	W
4.	O
5.	Y
6.	G
7.	T
8.	K
9.	L
10.	D
11.	F
12.	L
13.	M
14.	P
15.	T
16.	D
17.	T
18.	L
19.	N
20.	M

3. Letter Series

1.	L
2.	H
3.	P
4.	S
5.	KB
6.	RS
7.	SP
8.	HRE
9.	R
10.	G
11.	N
12.	C
13.	Y
14.	PA
15.	E
16.	W
17.	BR
18.	OTY
19.	S
20.	M

4. Letter Relationships

1.	OP
2.	RS
3.	GE
4.	JH
5.	WT
6.	UW
7.	XX
8.	RST
9.	ILK
10.	AC
11.	OV
12.	EIF
13.	YVU
14.	QP
15.	JR
16.	CEH
17.	BQ
18.	EEE
19.	QUO
20.	NOV

5. Codes

1.	REAR
2.	FILE
3.	BVTU
4.	XKEVQT
5.	FAIL
6.	LAUGH
7.	GROUND
8.	RACE
9.	RMIZ
10.	BLUE
11.	BRSPJ
12.	BROKE
13.	QZEIHQ
14.	QTXZ
15.	TZYX
16.	RYKL
17.	WINES
18.	GATE
19.	SOAP
20.	FCCD

6. Combining Words

1.	CARTRIDGE
2.	COTTON
3.	RATHER
4.	PLEASURE
5.	DETERMINE
6.	FORBID
7.	HERRING
8.	REASONABLE
9.	KIDNAP
10.	WITHOUT
11.	COVERING
12.	PAGEANT
13.	ORBIT
14.	WEEKEND
15.	MANAGE
16.	PASSWORD
17.	CABIN
18.	MESSAGE
19.	SOUP
20.	SAFEGUARD

7. Completing Words

1. ART
2. INK
3. ROW
4. HAT
5. MEN
6. PEN
7. ARE
8. NOR
9. PAN
10. EAR
11. HIM
12. AND
13. CAP
14. ROW
15. PET
16. BIN
17. LEG
18. FOR
19. SAT
20. PEN

8. Hidden Words

1. sent
2. hall
3. kind
4. rang
5. tall
6. them
7. prod
8. nice
9. edit
10. dumb
11. hero
12. sand
13. thin
14. echo
15. chin
16. mean
17. dove
18. mast
19. read
20. slim

9. Matching Words

1. SLAP
2. PART
3. RAIN
4. RIPE
5. CROP
6. SPEND
7. BLACK
8. DATE
9. PLAN
10. CRAB
11. LONE
12. BRAG
13. LISTS
14. PART
15. ABLE
16. TRAP
17. CRAM
18. LEGS
19. MAST
20. HOPED

10. Word Patterns

1. HAT
2. STEP
3. TIDE
4. GRIN
5. RUSTS
6. SAT
7. SAT
8. TIP
9. GRIN
10. FIGHT
11. BREAD
12. BELL
13. POND
14. LASS
15. ANT
16. PEN
17. KIN
18. SIT
19. LAKE
20. AND
21. LACE
22. SIDE
23. POKE
24. BIB
25. CAR

11. Word Change

1. MUST
2. SOLD
3. PINK
4. LIMP
5. TRIM
6. SLAY
7. WALL
8. CASH
9. TAPE
10. WORE
11. TOLL
    TELL
12. CARE
    MARE
13. DUST
    DUET
14. WING
    WIND
15. SLAM
    SLAY
16. TURN
    TORN
17. SOOT
    BOOT
18. HOME
    HOLE
19. BALL
    BALE
20. PRAY
    TRAY

12. Word Order

1. postbox & street
2. sunny & winter
3. injured & kind
4. escaping & frightened
5. short & young
6. at & in
7. huge & wild
8. won & entered
9. down & off
10. fruit & apple
11. victory & minute
12. fog & was
13. draw & game
14. history & survey
15. up & flash
16. postman & angry
17. silenced & heavy
18. holiday & crowded
19. equal & triangle
20. clown & the

13. Vocabulary Questions 1: Common Word

1. abolish
2. desert
3. part
4. border
5. difference
6. equal
7. fight
8. clip
9. withdraw
10. act
11. remove
12. minute
13. fragile
14. conceal
15. clear
16. change
17. file
18. hesitant
19. style
20. great

14. Vocabulary Questions 2: Opposites

1. generous & selfish
2. rigid & flexible
3. balanced & lopsided
4. commencement & termination
5. immense & diminutive
6. obscure & distinct
7. irritated & contented
8. accurate & inexact
9. unique & common
10. casual & careful
11. heroism & cowardice
12. pause & proceed
13. hinder & assist
14. drawback & benefit
15. ignorant & educated
16. blameless & guilty
17. extended & shortened
18. quiet & noisy
19. destroy & create
20. intact & damaged

15. Vocabulary Questions 3: Words Closest in Meaning

1. abundant & plentiful
2. admire & respect
3. kind & caring
4. alter & change
5. anger & wrath
6. catastrophe & misfortune
7. comfort & console
8. destroy & demolish
9. meagre & scanty
10. edge & rim
11. eject & expel
12. envy & resentment
13. flourish & thrive
14. guard & defend
15. image & copy
16. fair & just
17. lack & scarcity
18. glisten & glow
19. vague & unclear
20. disclose & divulge

16. Vocabulary Questions 4: Odd One Out

1. obstruct & hinder
2. partially & selection
3. challenge & inquiry
4. release & ignored
5. authorise & sanction
6. arrogant & conceited
7. advise & educate
8. restricted & confined
9. repel & antagonise
10. routine & order
11. surrender & submission
12. scarce & meagre
13. hasten & speed
14. ravine & gorge
15. exalt & honour
16. deceive & neglect
17. continue & unite
18. prejudiced & devious
19. captivate & conciliate
20. prototype & orignal

17. Sentence Connections

1. army & navy
2. trunk & stem
3. bat & racquet
4. coin & note
5. spot & stripe
6. slow & fast
7. trap & frill
8. quartet & trio
9. happy & sad
10. bean & leaf
11. foe & friend
12. delighted & miserable
13. three & four
14. surgery & court
15. cross & secure
16. ocean & river
17. fish & mouse
18. soul & sail
19. gold & oil
20. aircraft & ships

18. Number Series

1. 22
2. 23
3. 31
4. 21
5. 96
6. 2880
7. 8
8. 6
9. 8
10. 20
11. 24
12. 21
13. 25
14. 50
15. 121
16. 136
17. 3
18. 914
19. 18
20. 768

19. Number Substitution

1.
- i. C
- ii. C
- iii. C
- iv. C

2.
- i. C
- ii. B
- iii. A
- iv. B

3.
- i. A
- ii. A
- iii. C
- iv. D

4.
- i. D
- ii. E
- iii. A
- iv. A

5.
- i. D
- ii. A
- iii. E
- iv. A

6.
- i. B
- ii. D
- iii. E
- iv. D

20. Number Relationships

1. 23
2. 24
3. 32
4. 99
5. 3
6. 76
7. 60
8. 36
9. 105
10. 53
11. 48
12. 2
13. 10
14. 35
15. 4
16. 11
17. 10
18. 10
19. 28
20. 54

21. Matching Words and Symbols

1.
- i. BLAME
- ii. BLEED
- iii. BLADE
- iv. LABEL

2.
- i. LIVE
- ii. EVIL
- iii. VILE
- iv. VEIL

3.
- i. PEAL
- ii. PALE
- iii. LEAP

4.
- i. READ
- ii. REAR
- iii. AREA

5.
- i. DREAD
- ii. RADAR
- iii. DARED
- iv. DATED

6.
- i. DARED
- ii. DREAD
- iii. BREED
- iv. BARED

7.
- i. PLEAD
- ii. PALED
- iii. APPLE

8.
- i. SLIME
- ii. MILES
- iii. ISLES

22. Interpretation of Data

1.
- a) Bernard
- b) Colin
- c) Alan
- d) David

2.
- a) coffee & chocolate
- b) 1
- c) milk

3.
- a) Friday
- b) E
- c) Thursday
- d) Saturday
- e) Tuesday & Friday
- f) Saturday & Tuesday

4.
- a) E
- b) A
- c) D

5.
- a) Erica
- b) Bill
- c) Mint
- d) 1
- e) 1

6.
- a) ludo
- b) Ann
- c) Scrabble
- d) 3
- e) Ann

ANTHEM LEARNING BOOKS	
TITLE	ISBN
Anthem How To Do 11 + and 12+Verbal Reasoning:Technique and Practice	ISBN13: 978 0 85728 382 5 ISBN 10: 0 85728 382 0
Anthem Test Papers 11 + and 12+Verbal Reasoning Book 1	ISBN13: 978 0 85728 383 2 ISBN10: 0 85728 383 9
Anthem Test Papers 11 + and 12+Verbal Reasoning Book 2	ISBN13: 978 0 85728 385 6 ISBN 10: 0 85728 385 5
Anthem Short Revision Papers 11 + and 12+Verbal Reasoning Book 1	ISBN13: 978 0 85728 384 9 ISBN10: 0 85728 384 7
Anthem Short Revision Papers 11 + and 12+Verbal Reasoning Book 2	ISBN13: 978 0 85728 386 3 ISBN10: 0 85728 386 3

Anthem Junior English Book Preparatory Book	ISBN13: 978 0 85728 356 6 ISBN10: 0 85728 356 1
Anthem Junior English Book 1	ISBN13: 978 0 85728 358 0 ISBN10: 0 85728 358 8
Anthem Junior English Book 2	ISBN13: 978 0 85728 360 3 ISBN10: 0 85728 360 X
Anthem Junior English Book 3	ISBN13: 978 0 85728 362 7 ISBN10: 0 85728 362 6
Anthem English Book 1	ISBN13: 978 0 85728 364 1 ISBN10: 0 85728 364 2
Anthem English Book 2	ISBN13: 978 0 85728 366 5 ISBN10: 0 85728 366 9
Anthem English Book 3	ISBN13: 978 0 85728 368 9 ISBN10: 0 85728 368 5

Anthem Junior Mathematics Book 3	ISBN13: 978 0 85728 370 2 ISBN10: 0 85728 370 7
Anthem Junior Mathematics Book 3 Test Papers	ISBN13: 978 0 85728 372 6 ISBN10: 0 85728 372 3
Anthem Mathematics Book 1	ISBN13: 978 0 85728 373 3 ISBN10: 0 85728 373 1
Anthem Mathematics Book 1 Test Papers	ISBN13: 978 0 85728 375 7 ISBN10: 0 85728 375 8
Anthem Mathematics Book 2	ISBN13: 978 0 85728 376 4 ISBN10: 0 85728 376 6
Anthem Mathematics Book 2 Test Papers	ISBN13: 978 0 85728 378 8 ISBN10: 0 85728 378 2
Anthem Mathematics Book 3	ISBN13: 978 0 85728 379 5 ISBN10: 0 85728 379 0
Anthem Mathematics Book 3 Test Papers	ISBN13: 978 0 85728 381 8 ISBN10: 0 85728 381 2

VISIT WWW.ANTHEMPRESS.COM TO ORDER ONLINE.

Printed in Great Britain
by Amazon

64714196R00045